GRAND CANAL

A history of Venice

Doges, brigands and navigators
narrated by ancient rooms

arsenale et editrice

Editorial co-ordination
Arsenale Editore

Text
Giovanni Cavarzere

English Translation
Peter Eustace

Photography
Mark E. Smith
Archivio Arsenale

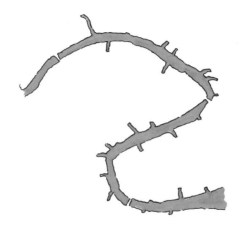

Canal Grande

A history of Venice

Doges, brigands and navigators
narrated by ancient rooms

First Edition January 2009

© **ARSENALE EDITRICE**

Arsenale Editore Srl
Via Ca' Nova Zampieri, 29
37057 - San Giovanni Lupatoto (Verona)
Italy

Introduction

The Grand Canal is the majestic setting of a colourful drama – the history of the Serene Republic of Venice, based on timid first steps, magnificent events, sublime nobility and gossip, pride and subterfuge, high politics and masked balls, trade and piracy.

In Venice "the Dominant", aristocratic families – from the most ancient to those that paid immense sums of money to rise to the nobility – built symbols of their power in form of sumptuous palaces. Famous architects, highly-skilled decorators and magnificent painters all contributed in different epochs to give material form to the pride of the Venetian aristocracy.

These palaces were where the fate of the city was decided, where murders and marriages were plotted, where magnificent feasts were held in honour of monarchs and princes from all over Europe, where some collected works of art and others sought ecclesiastical privileges. Every palace boasts a hidden history among its stones, a decisive episode for the city or an event that illuminated the private life of the nobleman.

This book aims to narrate some of the most significant histories through masonry and documents, well-known and obscure figures, navigators, traders, politicians and architects. A story going back more than one thousand years...

The age of splendour

Ca' Da Mosto

Alvise, the most famous offspring of the noble Da Mosto family, was born in this palace in 1432. By 1454 he had already gained much experience in sea travels and Marco Zeno took him on board his galley setting sail for Flanders. A storm forced him to seek refuge in Gibraltar and this fortuitous event changed his life: he met the heir to throne of Portugal, Henry the Navigator, who invited him to take command of one of his ships to explore the Atlantic coast of Africa. Alvise departed on 22 March 1455, stopping at Madera and then at the Canary Isles before reaching the Senegal estuary. Here, he met Genoan Antoniotto Usodimare, another explorer, and together they reached the Gambia estuary. Alvise – as he personally wrote in his records – wanted to sail up the river, but his crew was not very enthusiastic and the natives were rather inhospitable. The noble Venetian renounced the feat – but only for the time being: the following year, he returned to the area and this time his travels brought two results that turned him into a discoverer: he was the first European to see the Capo Verde Islands and, as well as sailing up the Gambia for 70 miles, he also reached the estuary of the Rio Grande and the Bissagos Islands. On his return, he settled in Portugal, at Lagos, where he carried out trade with Africa. He returned to Venice in 1460, to this palace, and five years later married noblewoman Betta Venier. In 1473, he took part in the defence of Cattaro, besieged by the Turks, and later took command of a fleet of trading galleys sailing to Alexandria. He died in 1488 without leaving heirs.

In XVII century, since the family had died out, the palace became a hotel: the "White Lion Inn". Emperor Joseph II stayed here twice during official visits in 1769 and 1775. The most memorable guest, however, was Grand Duke Paul Petrovic, the future Czar Paul I, with his wife Maria Feodorovna, in 1782: it was the pretext that saw the aristocratic families compete to organise feasts and performances – probably the most sumptuous of the 1700s.

Fondaco dei Turchi

In the early 1200s, Giacomo Palmieri, consul of the free city of Pesaro, was deposed and banished from the city following the defeat of his faction. Palmieri never returned to "his" Pesaro: he settled in Venice, then already a dominant trading power, and to establish his name commissioned a sumptuous palace that could by no means pass unnoticed.

The objective was achieved with such precision that the palace was noted by the Republic itself: in 1381, the doge required a Venetian residence worthy of his precious ally, Nicolò d'Este, Marquis of Ferrara, who had helped him during the War of Chioggia against the Genoans. Although old Palmieri had written in his will that the palace should never be sold, his three heirs did not hesitate and, for the astonishing sum of ten thousand gold ducats, sold the palace to the Serene Republic, which in turn immediately gave it to Marquis d'Este. The gift symbolised the alliance between the two states and was thus involved in the turbulent history of Italian politics: when, in 1509, the Este family joined the anti-Venetian League of Cambrai, the Republic of St. Mark confiscated the palace, first leasing and then making a gift of it to Pope Julius II. Later, in 1527, Ferrara made a new alliance with Venice and the palace was returned to the Este family. In 1602, Cesare d'Este sold it to Cardinal Aldobrandini, who in turn sold it in 1618 to Antonio Priuli, who was elected doge in the same year. The palace took its

Grand Canal: a history of Venice

present name in XVII century when the Venetian government decided to offer the Turks a public hotel, where they could stay for trading purposes; the Turks were obliged to reside here during their stay in Venice and had to observe a strict evening curfew: it was a way of protecting them and their goods at the same time as keeping them under control. After the War of Candia (1645-1669), trade with the Ottoman Empire became increasingly marginal and the payment for lodgings of Turkish merchants – that is, all merchants of all nationalities as subjects of the Sultan (especially Bosnians and Albanians in Venice) – no longer sufficed to cover the maintenance of the palace, so much so that in 1732 a part of the building collapsed. In 1838, the palace was purchased by Antonio Busetto, a "palazzinaro", who renovated it to create luxury apartments.

The Fondaco, by now almost uninhabitable, was the home at the time to the last Turkish merchant still active in Venice. His name was Saddo Drisdi – and was evicted so that restructuring work could begin. In 1860, Venice City Council, then under the dominion of Austria, purchased the palace for 80 thousand florins. Today, it is home to the Natural History Museum.

Fondaco dei Turchi *was restored in 1869 in accordance with the theories of the period and everything that time and neglect had cancelled was restored on the basis of the views of painters and engravers.*

Palazzo Corner Loredan Piscopia

In 1366, Cyprus was ruled by Pietro II of Lusignan, a penniless and thus poorly armed monarch: the island was therefore easy prey and rather tempting for the Ottoman empire. Pietro had no other choice but to set sail for the Republic of the Winged Lion – a determined enemy of the Turks – for what would today be called a *fund-raising tour* but in reality was merely the visit by a poor relative to a wealthy cousin. He was welcomed by Federico Corner, a nobleman who also boasted other very solid credentials: he was the main tax-payer in the Serene Republic – the wealthiest man in a city of very wealthy merchants. Federico welcomed the King of Cyprus to his palace as an honoured guest and gave him what he was looking for: an enormous loan. To repay his debt, Pietro II decided to satisfy both the glory and the munificence of Federico Corner: he awarded him the title of Knight of the Sword and donated to him the Cypriot domain of Piscopia. Here, the Corner family had rights to grow and refine sugar cane with total exemption of customs duties and taxes. Sooner or later, however, things were set to change: in 1571, Cyprus was conquered by the Turks and the Corner family lost its profitable business on the island. The fortunes of the family were laid even lower by the last-but-one heir, Giovanni Battista, who decided to marry a commoner, Zanetta Bonis. The marriage was scandalous for aristocratic society, so much so that the "Avogaria di Comun" – usually rather generous – denied aristocratic status to the couple's two sons: one of the twelve "Old Families" thus suffered the disgrace of seeing its very ancient lineage cancelled. The noble Corner did not give up hope and appealed to the Senate and the Main Council to obtain at least inclusion in the aristocracy against payment. Despite his munificent offer of money, the government on this occasion decided to set

an example and the request was repealed. Yet Giovanni Battista himself was determined not to give up and, in 1664, his fourth appeal was at last accepted. Yet Corner was still not satisfied and decided also to emancipate the parent-child relationship: as well as two sons, Corner also had a daughter, Elena Lucrezia, who had a specific talent for study. In the noble families of the times, women were destined to learn at most how to behave in society and then suffer an arranged marriage. Elena Lucrezia, on the other hand, thanks to the support of her father, was allowed to study and even attended the University of Padua. In 1677, she wanted to take a degree in theology but the indignant Bishop of Padua forbade it; the year after, she gained a degree in philosophy – the first women in history to achieve this title.

*Built in the 1200s by the Boccasi family originally from Parma, **Palazzo Corner Loredan Piscopia** later passed into the hands of the noble Zane family and lastly to one of the oldest Venetian aristocratic houses: the Corner. This family was so rich that it could even make loans to monarchs in other countries.*

Palazzo Dandolo Farsetti

Built end XII-early XIII century, this palace was the residence of Andrea Dandolo, doge from 1343 to 1354. The Dandolo family was one of the twelve "Old Families", by no coincidence known as "apostolic", whose representatives in 697 A.D.

elected the first doge. In 1204, Enrico Dandolo, ninety and almost blind, commanded the Venetian fleet during the conquest of Byzantium. Andrea was not a direct descendent of Enrico; he was not a "legendary" doge like his forebear and was not even particularly fortunate: he was called upon to govern the empire during the plague, that took the lives of three-fifths of the Venetians, and was then immediately presented by a doubtful war against the Genoans, won "at the negotiating table" because of internal conflicts among the Ligurians, while the result in the field was far from favourable. The Genoan war also saw the end of his intimate friendship with Petrarch, who he thought was too favourable to the Visconti, who were allied with Genoa. Such political and family burdens probably affected his health and he died at only 48 – of a broken heart, it was said. In 1679, the palace was sold to Anton Francesco Farsetti, a Tuscan who joined the Main Council (the "parliament" of the Serene Republic whose members where exclusively aristocrats) only in 1664: the oldest and most dignified ancient Venetian family sold the palace to a *parvenu*. The Farsetti were by no means wealthy social climbers but were very interested in culture. Abbot Filippo Vincenzo filled the palace with chalk models of the finest Greek sculptures commissioned all over Europe. Assolda was also a sculptor who taught the most promising young artists – and it was precisely here that Antonio Canova took the first steps in his extraordinary career. Tommaso Giuseppe, his cousin, collected a splendid library, which was bequeathed to the Marciana. Unfortunately for them, even the Farsetti grew old and took up the vices of the old noble families: after building a fortune, it was then thrown away. In their case, the fortune was lost by Antonio Francesco, ironically named after his forebear who first bought the palace. On the death of this father, he attempted to sell all the works of art but was prevented by the inquisitors of the Republic. After the fall of the Serene Republic, however, no one prevented him selling everything off to Tsar Paul I, only to die in poverty in St. Petersburg. The Austrians then purchased these sculpture models from the Russians and gave then to the Venetian Academy, while the widow of Antonio Francesco re-purchased the palace as the creditor of her dowry – which her husband had also squandered.

Lagoon Gothic

Ca' d'Oro

This palace was built in the first half of XV century by Marino Contarini, who in 1431 engaged a French painter, Giovanni Charlier, to gilt the statues, cornices and other details of the facade. Hence the name of the building that, even in the colourful Venice of the 1400s, could hardly have passed unnoticed. The palace became so famous that Pietro, the son of Marino Contarini's second marraige, was nicknamed *"Ca' d'Oro"*. The property was subsequently and progressively fragmented, so much so that in 1808 a certain Giacomo Pezzi bought it as "a ruined building" In the middle of the century it was purchased by Russian Prince Alexander Troubetzkoi as a gift for Maria Taglioni, the very famous *étoile*. Taglioni was a "collector" of Venetian palaces: when Ca' d'Oro was given to her she already owned the Venetian-Byzantine palace where she lived, a building by Longhena, the Giustinian Lolin and the Corner Spinelli palaces. The Russian Prince, guilty of a weakness for the Hapsburgs, had been exiled to Siberia. It was whispered that Tsar Nicholas I had pardoned him only thanks to the insistence of Taglioni, his lover; Ca' d'Oro was therefore Troubetzkoi's gift to the woman who

*The monumental staircase and the precious well-head in the inner courtyard of **Ca' d'Oro** were returned to their original positions following inauspicious "restoration" in the 1800s.*

saved him. Unfortunately, the Prince decided to restore the building, precisely in a century when restoration was synonymous with total lack of respect and of bungled reconstruction. This disfigurement was the work of engineer Giambattista Meduna, who removed pillars and cornices, destroyed floors and balustrades and revolutionised the ground plan, following his own personal idea of what a Venetian Gothic palace should look like. He even dismantled the exceptionally beautiful outside staircase designed by Matteo Raverti and offered the precious well-head by Bartolomeo Bon for sale. If today we can still admire these artefacts, the merit goes to Giorgio Franchetti, who saved the staircase, re-purchased the well-head and repaired the numerous tamperings. Today, the building is home to a significant art gallery.

Ca' Foscari

Among the many palaces overlooking the Grand Canal, Ca' Foscari can be considered as the *par ex-*

cellence "palace of power". Owned by Bernardo Giustinian, in 1429 is was purchased by the Serene Republic as a gift for Gianfrancesco Gonzaga, Lord of Mantua, at the time a precious ally. After one of the rapid turn-abouts the rulers of Italy often resorted to for survival, the Republic decided to regain possession of it to present it as a gift to Francesco Sforza, at that time the mercenary commander of the Venetian troops. The continual roundabout of alliances that characterised the period at one point must have persuaded the Serene Republic to renounce such gifts, continually offered only to be immediately confiscated, and in 1452 the palace was put up for auction. The fortunate winner was Francesco Foscari, doge of Venice since 1423: the suspicion that the auction was "rigged" is therefore not entirely out of place. Doge Foscari completely demolished the facade in order to rebuild it in the Gothic style then fashionable. Francesco Foscari was the longest-reigning doge and one of the great doges in history:

he decided to extend the Republic inland in order to create the largest possible territory between Venice and its powerful neighbours. Venice managed to expand its boundaries as far as Bergamo: this involved four wars against Milan and considerable expenditure, but his approach achieved the desired results. Unfortunately for him, political success was matched by private disappointments: his son Jacopo was rather reckless, as sometimes happens among the children of great men, and was exiled for bribery. On his return, he was accused – this time unfairly – of having killed one of the magistrates who had sentenced him, the nobleman Almorò Donà. He was then sent to Crete and none of Francesco's political intrigues managed to secure his return: two years later, Jacopo died in exile. This sad story later inspired Lord Byron to write his drama *The Two Foscari*, which Verdi set to music in 1844. Even the political career of the great doge came to a bad end: in 1457, the Council of Ten forced him to abdicate because of poor health, and he died three days after resigning.

The palace remained in the possession of the Foscari family until the fall of the Serene Republic in 1797, and then was home to a long sequence of princes: Ferdinand and Maximilian of Austria in 1579, Ernest Augustus Duke of Brunswick in 1686, the Margrave of Brandenburg in 1687, King Ferdinand IV of Denmark in 1709 and the Elector of Saxony in 1739. The most popular of all these guests, however, was Henry III of Valois, King of France and Poland, who stayed in the palace in 1574. The Serene Republic offered numerous honours to the foreign monarch that lasted several days: he was met in Marghera by a gondola and escorted to Murano by 60 senators, each of whom in a gondola draped with precious fabrics and oriental carpets. On arrival in Murano, Henry III was welcomed by the doge, Alvise Mocenigo, with 40 young nobleman as his personal escort.

The doge took the king aboard the galley of the Capitan of the Gulf with its crew of 400 rowers dressed in yellow and blue taffeta for the trip to San Nicolò del Lido. The Republic had installed a Triumphal Arch designed by Andrea Palladio and decorated by Il Veronese, Tintoretto and Aliense. Henry III was then taken to Palazzo Foscari on a bucentaur where, beneath the windows for the entire night, a floating furnace was operated so that the king could admire the skill of craftsmen in working blown glass.

*Today, despite also having been used as a barracks by the Austrians, **Ca' Foscari** is the main head office of Venice University.*

Palazzo Bembo

This imposing Gothic palace belonged to one of the most illustrious families of the Republic, one of the "Old Families" already ennobled before IX century. Yet only one Bembo was ever the doge of the Serene Republic – Giovanni, who reigned 1615-1618 and was also a brave admiral. At the time, the Adriatic was infested by the Uscocchi – Christian refugees from Bosnia and Dalmatia by then under Turkish rule – who were protected by the Hapsburgs. They made a living as pirates and were used and financed by the Austrians as warriors on the frontier with the Ottomans and to disturb the trade and dominion of the Serene

Republic in the Adriatic. After defeating the pirates in battle, Giovanni took the prisoners to Venice – the Republic then displayed their heads in St. Mark's Squares for the joy of citizens. In turn, the pirates captured a Venetian commander and held a fine banquet during which they ate the heart of the unfortunate man. The question was settled in 1618 with an offensive in Friuli against the Austrians that achieved more of a diplomatic than a military victory: the Hapsburgs agreed to deport the Uscocchi to the hinterland of Croatia and to burn their ships.

The most worthy son of the family was Cardinal Pietro Bembo, of the branch owning the palace, where he was born in 1470. Pietro, however, was something of a vagabond: as a young man he studied Greek in Messina and completed his studies in Padua. He was then a guest of Lucrezia Borgia in Ferrara, where it is claimed he was her lover. It is nevertheless true that, despite having taken up an ecclesiastical career, he never denied himself carnal joys and even had a family. When he moved to Rome in 1512, following Giuliano de' Medici, he met Ambrogina Faustina della Torre. The meeting with "Morosina" – as he nicknamed her – culminated in a relationship that lasted until her death and issued three children: Lucilio, Torquato and Elena. All this did not prevent him becoming the secretary of Pope Leo X. In 1521, after the death of the Pope, he moved to Padua, where they lived as man and wife. In 1529, he became the official historiographer of the Serene Republic and a year later the librarian of Marciana. "Morosina" died in 1535 and Pietro dedicated himself more seriously to his ecclesiastical career and was eventually made a cardinal.

Palazzo Bernardo

The history of Palazzo Bernardo may not be unique but it certainly is rather particular: it was

built as the home for two families of the Bernardo dynasty but soon after came to used as a
temporary residence for dignitaries during official visits. The couple who inaugurated this "luxury inn" comprised Francesco Sforza, the future
ruler of Milan, and Bianca Visconti. They stayed
here early in 1442, shortly after their marriage,
and their visit was also the first occasion when
the palace was mentioned, so that it is assumed
it was built only a little earlier. For most of the
time, the Bernardo occupied the entire palace
but when the Serene Republic had important
guests they hastily packed their bags and moved
to a single floor. In any case, the dynasty certainly had a vein of madness, at least judging
from the last will and testament of Senator Pietro Bernardo dated 1515. It was described by
Giuseppe Tassini in his 1800s *Venetian Curiosities*:
"He ordered that, immediately after his death,
he should be washed in the most exquisite vine-

*Palazzo Bernardo is
a full-scale "palace for
two": since it was used
by two families, it was
built with two noble
floors, two doors for
access from the canal,
two doors for access
from the street, two
courtyards and two
staircases.*

gar and then anointed with a musk, *pel valsente* costing 40 ducats, by three doctors whose fee would be three fine 'zecchini' each; that he should be buried with aloe and others spices in a lead coffin where he could lie comfortably, that this coffin should be enclosed by another large coffin in cypress wood, so well sealed and tarred as to be impossible to open except by breaking it; that he be placed in a marble ark worth 600 ducats, the face of which should be carved with eight hexameters proclaiming his deeds in capital letters legible at a distance of 25 feet, paying the poet one 'zecchino' every two verses; that the top of the ark be carved with the Eternal Father and Pietro Bernardo himself kneeling, of such dimensions as to seem at a distance of 25 feet men of great stature; that, ultimately, a book of 800 verses should celebrate the glories of his family, comprising seven psalms imitating those of David and other orations, to be sung every first Sunday of the month by 20 friars, at the break of dawn, in front of his tomb." The Bernardo family was not crazy enough to satisfy the megalomania of Pietro, yet in any case at least they did erect his tomb: the funerary monument is still visible in the Frari church.

Palazzo Contarini Fasan

Despite being built at the end of the 1400s, when the Renaissance in Italy had already conquered all spaces, the style of the building yielded nothing to "modernity". It was owned by a Contarini – the family boasting the most doges, as many as eight – who was so fond of hunting that he was nicknamed "fasan" (pheasant).

It is actually a rather small palace, almost a flourishing *pied-à-terre* strictly in the late Gothic style. Perhaps this is why legend has it that it was the home of Desdemona, the unfortunate wife of Shakespeare's Othello.

Palazzo Falier Canossa

This palace was refurbished in the 1800s but was originally built XIV century and until quite recently was the home of the very ancient Falier family. The family provided Venice with three doges. It was during the rule of the first of the doges, Vitale, that the body of St. Mark was rediscovered. The relic had disappeared in June 1094; the Venetians were so shocked that they took to continual fasting and prayer until a miracle took place: on 25 June the doge, the bishop, nobles and commoners met in the Basilica for yet another supplication, when the Saint's arm emerged from a column in the nave to indicate the place where his body could be found. The second Falier doge, Ordelaf, died in battle beneath the walls of Zara in 1118. The third was the infamous Marino, who in 1355 plotted a coup and, on being discovered, was beheaded on one of the staircases of the Ducal Palace. Thereafter, the family never again had the honour of becoming a doge, although another member attempted to reverse its reputation as the destroyer of Venetian institutions: in 1492, Francesco Falier proposed that the Republic should donate 100 ducats a year to nobles fallen on poverty. He was immediately condemned to perpetual exile in Cyprus; nevertheless, he was soon pardoned and allowed to return to his palace.

*The originality of the facade of **Palazzo Falier Canossa** arises from the two inside balconies, known as "liagò", at the sides. They are not two imaginative additions of an eccentric architect but the re-utilisation of two existing structures right from the original project.*

Palazzo Giustinian

Palazzo Giustinian is made up of two distinct buildings, which were joined in the mid-1400s. A fusion of facades that can well be said to "keep up appearances": while the view from the Grand Canal may give the illusion of a single building, in reality there are two separate entities.

The Giustinian noble family claimed descent from Emperor Justinian, naturally because of the similarity of these names. This "Old Family" risked dying out in XII century and was only saved by a "miracle". All the males died during the expedition sent in 1171 by the Serene Republic against the Byzantine Emperor Manuel Comnenus, some in battle and others of the plague. The only surviving heir, Nicolò, was unfortunately unable to help matters: he had become a monk and lived in the Benedictine monastery of San Nicolò al Lido. Desperate remedies for desperate needs: Pope Alexander III in person allowed Nicolò to break his vow of chastity and to continue the family the by-now former friar married Anna, the daughter of doge Vitale II Michiel. Following the disastrous outcome of the expedition against the Byzantines, a group of trouble-makers murdered Vitale II but even in mourning his daughter Anna completed her task of ensuring continuity of the Giustinian line. Fortunately, the couple were very fertile and their marriage bore five sons. Having done his duty, however, Nicolò resumed his religious life and retired definitively to the monastery at the Lido. His wife Anna imitated him: she took vows and went to live in the Benedictine convent of Sant'Ariano, an island in the lagoon near Torcello.

Palazzo Giustinian Morosini

Modernised in 1474, the palace was already home to a branch of the Giustinian family in XIV century. Like the other palace owned by the family described here, Palazzo Giustinian, it involves two separate buildings that were only merged at a later date:. In this case, however, the "merger" is not only external: the two buildings were combined into a single, larger residence. It was purchased by the Morosini in the 1600s and it is curious to note that the only doge of the Giustinian family, Marcantonio, reigned 1684-1688 – when Francesco Morosini regained for the Serene Republic the territories fallen into the hands of the Turks. The name of the palace therefore recalls the last glorious moment of the Republic of St. Mark before its long decline. In the 1800s, it was converted into one of the most elegant hotels in the city, the Hotel Europa whose guests included Marcel Proust, René de Chateaubriand and Stendhal.

Palazzo Loredan dell'Ambasciatore

It was built around mid-XV century for the Loredan family. A rather fanciful genealogical tree traces the origins of the noble family even to Muzio Scevola, but there is no need to rely merely only legends to emphasise its central role in the history of Venice: Loredan doges and warriors are the protagonists of many significant episodes. Their fame, however, is also linked with an arrogant and vindictive character. The palace takes its name from the profitable deal closed around 1754 by its owner, Francesco Loredan, doge from 1752 to 1762. The Imperial Court of Austria requested the palace as the home for its Embassy, proposing a leasing contract of 29 years. Francesco was perhaps a little unwilling to agree but could hardly deny the proposition for political reasons. How did he solve the problem? With a proposal that the doge assumed to be unacceptable to the Austrians: the palace would be granted provided that the 29 year lease was paid in full and immediately. There's more: necessary restoration work would be entirely sustained by the Austrian court. Incredible as it may seem, the Austrians accepted and Francesco found himself with a financial fortune and a completely renovated palace.

Palazzo Morosini Brandolin

The palace was built in the first half XV century by the San Cassiano branch of the Morosini family. It has long since been split into private apartments: in the 1800s, the third floor was demolished, while the second floor was split in two to create "middle class" homes that were easier to rent or sell. The two entrances on the ground floor are an 1800s reconstruction, while the magnificent Gothic hexaphores on the main floors are originals, as are the other windows.

The Morosini were members of the exclusive circle of "apostolic" families – the 12 noble dynasties traditionally claimed as taking part in 697 in the election of the first doge, Paoluccio Anafesto. The family boasts as many as four doges and twenty-seven procurators of St. Mark – surpassed in this particular "ranking" only by the Mocenigo (seven doges and twenty-five procurators). The most illustrious member of the Morosini family is without doubt Francesco, the hero of Candia (then the capital of Crete). The island – a dominion of the Serene Republic since 1204 – was conquered by the Turks in 1645; the Venetians retreated to Candia (modern Iraklion), where they were besieged. The last commander of this stronghold was the 28 year-old Admiral of the Fleet of St. Mark, Francesco Morosini. The Venetians withstood the siege for 24 years - but were forced to surrender in September 1669. The Turks were so impressed by the courage of the defenders that they allowed them all to return home without harm. Nevertheless, in 1687, the bellicose Morosini took his revenge by re-conquering Morea (the Peloponnesus) following several naval victories. He was elected doge in 1688 while still engaged in a siege. He found it hard to settle in Venice – he was far too accustomed to military life and much less to the intrigues of the nobility – so that, despite his election as doge, in 1690 he also resumed his Admiral's role and departed again with the fleet. He won other battles but was by then too old for the military life style. He died without ever seeing Venice again in Nauplia in 1694.

Palazzo Morosini Sagredo

Palazzo Morosini Sagredo was at the centre of famliy litigation that prevented its restoration – which is why we can still today admire the Gothic style of its facade: it combines the austere XIII century Gothic with the more decorative style of XIV century.

Gherardo Sagredo, procurator of St. Mark, dictated his last will and testament here in 1738: the palace was bequeathed to the wealthiest branch of the family at the time of his death. The procurator held the prestige of the family in the highest regard and the palace was its most visible symbol; by bequeathing it to his richest relatives, he ensured that money would be available to renovate the facade. He had personally commissioned the design by Tommaso Temanza, a disciple of Bernardino Zendrini, himself the designer of the Murazzi. Nevertheless, while he was alive, Gherardo revolutionised interiors in accordance with the fashion of the time. An inaccuracy in his will, however, was the basis for litigation between his heirs: what exactly did "the wealthiest branch of the family" effectively mean? On the basis of what criteria? His will of-

Palazzo Morosini Sagredo was argued about for sixty years by different branches of the family. Litigation only finished in 1797 – the same year that the Serene Republic came to an end. Like many other aristocratic families, the Sagredo also suffered ruin and were obliged to sell the art collection and all the furniture.

fered no such definition. When the Sagredo family of Santa Ternita finally won the dispute, the Serene Republic was on the point of capitulation and even the "wealthiest members of the family" were no longer able to finance a task of such dimensions. In any case, Gherardo wanted a palace in line with his own times – so that even Temanza's facade was already an old-fashioned anachronism. Gherardo's dream of *grandeur* remains only in the frescoes by Pietro Longhi flanking the main staircase: they are the only frescoes by this artist, an exception that testifies to the status and reputation of the Sagredo.

Palazzo Pisani "Moretta"

Built by the Bembo family in XV century, the palace was only purchased by the Pisani in 1629 – who were involved in the late-1700s in a memorable court case. The founder of the family, Nicolò Pisani, had two sons: Bertucci (Alberto) and Almorò (Ermolao). Bertucci founded the "Dal Banco" branch of the family – so-named after its banking and mercantile interests; Almorò founded the "Santo Stefano", "Santa Maria

Zobenigo" and "Moretta" family branches (the latter because so many male descendents were named Almorò). Francesco Pisani "Moretta", the last of the family, died in 1737 and left everything to his only daughter, Chiara. Chiara in the meantime had married Girolamo, of the "Dal Banco" branch of the Pisani family: yet the testaments of certain Pisani properties in short meant that they could only be inherited by family members born of legitimate marriage and entitled to be members of the Main Council. The choice of Chiara was plainly her father's only choice: the family could only hold on to its assets if she married a Pisani. Chiara and Girolamo had two sons – Pietro and Vettor – but unfortunately for their mother the second son made a mess of things: he fell in love with a commoner, Teresa Dalla Vedova, and married her in secret. When Chiara discovered this ruse, she disclaimed poor Teresa as her daughter-in-law and the State Inquisitors sent her to a convent. Yet Teresa was pregnant and gave birth to a son that the father banished from Venice. The powerful family also managed to have the marriage annulled by the ecclesiastic courts. The Pisani pretended that nothing had happened, while Teresa remarried and ensured a good upbringing for her son with Vettor, who she named Pietro. The boy was well-disposed, well-educated and especially determined to reclaim his birthright: the Pisani inheritance. In 1775, he began legal proceedings with famous lawyers – delighted as ever to take up "succulent" litigation cases – where the Pisani were represented by Pietro, procurator of St. Mark and the uncle of the same name as the youngster. The Quarantìa (the supreme court of the Republic) sentenced in favour of the young man, awarding him possession of the palace, various other assets and the title of Count of Bagnolo. On his death in 1847, Palazzo Pisani

The 1700s interiors of **Palazzo Pisani Moretta** are in an excellent state of conservation and the magnificent chandeliers in Murano glass still emanate the warm light of candles: electrical lighting has never been installed in the palace.

"Moretta" was inherited by his son, Vettor Daniele, who in turn left it to one of his three daughters, married to Count Giusti del Giardino. Today, the palace is owned by their heirs.

Even if she made life hard for her grandson Pietro, grandmother Chiara certainly had excellent taste: her father Francesco, after having saved and scrimped to save the family heritage, allowed his daughter to renovate the interiors of the palace: she commissioned the imposing main staircase (1742), designed by Andrea Tirali, and the fresco by Tiepolo depicting the meeting between Mars and Venus (1746).

A late Renaissance

Ca' Dario

In 1479, Giovanni Dario, an important diplomat of the Serene Republic, managed to sign an unexpected peace agreement with Mahomet II, sovereign of the Turks. The Republic rewarded him with the donation of land at Noventa Padovana and an impressive sum of money. Giovanni invested the "ducats" to purchase the palace on the Grand Canal and commissioned architect Pietro Lombardo to embellish it. The result is a magnificent jewel, where even the interiors resemble a fairy-tale. When Giovanni died, the palace was inherited by his only daughter, Marietta, married to a Barbaro. Soon after, the Barbaro family suffered bankruptcy and poor Marietta died of a broken heart. This was the first of a series of economic setbacks and violent deaths accompanying the owners of this building: in the 1800s, Arbid Abdoll, a wealthy Armenian dealer in precious stones, bought it and then immediately ruined his finances; the English academic Rawdon Brown, who bought the palace in 1938, committed suicide in his room together with his companion; American Charles Briggs fled from Venice in the wake of gossip about his homosexuality and, on arrival in Mexico, saw his companion also commit suicide. In 1970, Count Filippo Giordano delle Lanze was murdered by his lover, an 18 year old Croatian sailor, who was in turned murdered in London, where he had sought refuge; in 1981, soon after purchase, the manager of The Who, Christopher Lambert, committed suicide by jumping from the staircase of the London home of his mother; businessman Fabrizio Ferrari then bought it and soon after lost everything, including his sister who died in a mysterious and un-witnessed car accident. Lastly, the next owner, financier Raul

*Although admired for its original gracefulness, **Ca' Dario** nevertheless has a sad reputation associated with the terrible deaths of some of its owners.*

Gardini, took his life in 1993 in not very clear circumstances following his involvement in corruption enquiries. It was only in 2006, after 13 years, that the Ferruzzi Group managed to sell the property to an American trust for 8 million euros.

Ca' Dolfin Manin

The palace was built by Jacopo Sansovino around 1536 to a commission by Marco Giovanni Dolfin, procurator of St. Mark. Vasari noted that the noble Dolfin family paid 30 thousand ducats for the design and construction of the new residence. Before this palace was built, the site had a number of smaller buildings – always owned by the family – which then decided that it was high time to demonstrate to everyone its new, high social status.
This project was not so astonishing for its facade but for its "Roman" courtyard – that was unfor-

tunately demolished in the late-1700s to make way for a more functional setting for the requirements of the new owner. Period chronicles tell us that this courtyard was home to performances by the "Compagnia degli Accesi", one of the most important "Calza" theatre groups. These theatrical companies were founded in the 1400s and were so-named after the colours of the hosiery worn by their actors, who were generally young aristocrats: the Serene Republic was governed by old men and a career in politics could only begin at 40 - so, in the meantime, there was room for enjoyment. In 1564, Andrea Palladio built for the "Accesi" a memorable stage setting precisely for the courtyard of Palazzo Dolfin: "a beautiful stage resembling a city, with fine columns and other perspectives delightful to see", wrote Francesco Sansovino. In 1602, the Dolfin family died out and the palace changed hands until it was split

Ca' Dolfin Manin is a perfect model of monumental architecture in the 1500s, imposing yet at the same time airy, with a broad colonnade and two noble floors with many windows.

into rented apartments. Lodovico Manin, the last doge of the Serene Republic, managed to buy and restore it in 1787. The project was completed in 1801, when Lodovico had become "just another citizen". Even such an upstanding and generous man could not alone have saved the republic after a century of political inertia: in 1797, when the French arrived, he announced to the Main Council: "Tonight we are not even safe in our own beds". The palace was owned by the Manin until 1867, when it became the regional head offices of the National Bank of the Kingdom of Italy (today Bank of Italy).

Palazzo Balbi

"One of the hardest things to find in Venice is a rich Balbi" says an old proverb – a saying belied by the palace named after this family. The family never gave Venice a doge and none of its members ever held key roles in the Serene Republic: perhaps this is why Venice began to think that the Balbi, despite their ancient family heritage, never gained important positions because of a lack of money. In any case, Niccolò Balbi in the late 1500s decided to build a palace *where the Canal turns* – in other words, where the Grand Canal opens into St. Mark's Square, perhaps and precisely to disprove the family's reputation. Tassini's *Venetian Curiosities* narrates a particular anecdote: "The gentleman once lived in a rented home not far away and having innocently forgot to pay his dues, one fine day, as he made his way to the Council, he crossed paths with the owner, who brusquely demanded payment. Niccolò paid his debt but nevertheless terminated the lease and issued orders that the new palace be built; in the meantime, he and his family lived in a large vessel moored thereby that was so enormous that it obscured the home of the person who had been so rude to him in the street". It seems that Niccolò was wealthy enough to build a sumptuous palace on the Grand Canal but nevertheless preferred to pay rent! Rather than lacking funds, we should perhaps assume he was somewhat tight-fisted. The gorgeous new palace was designed by Alessandro Vittoria from the Trentino area – built in just nine years so that Niccolò and his family could abandon the vessel where they lived as soon as possible. The building was owned by the noble family until 1887, when it was sold to Michelangelo Guggenheim, an antiquarian who embellished the rooms with an impressive collection of works of art. In 1925, it was purchased by SADE (Adriatic Electricity Company) which, unfortunately, in 1953 commissioned disgraceful and violent restoration of the interiors to convert the building to needs of a modern company: one of the two monumental staircases was even demolished. In 1971, the palace was acquired by the Veneto Region; this time, it was properly restored and is now home to the regional council.

Palazzo Barbarigo della Terrazza

The facade of the palace overlooks Rio San Polo; it takes it name from the large terrace reflected in the Grand Canal, the only original feature of an otherwise very plain building. The Barbarigo were one of the "new" Venetian noble families that achieved this status after X century prior to the so-called "closure" enacted by the Council in 1297, when the Republic of St. Mark became an oligarchy and effectively blocked accession by new families to its higher ranks. It is one of the so-called "ducal families" – one of the sixteen noble houses that monopolised the election of the doge from 1382 to 1612. This family boasts two doges – brothers Marco and Agostino: The former was Doge 1485-1486, the latter 1486-1501. It is said that the family surname derives from a forebear,

*It seems that the terrace of **Palazzo Barbarigo** only arose because of a lack of money that prevented the building of the left wing.*

Arrigo, who in 880 took part in a battle against the Saracens, taking home with him the beards of six Moors he personally killed. This is apparently confirmed by the six black beards included in the family coat of arms. While this is obviously a legend, the Barbarigo were nevertheless a warlike family. The most illustrious member of the family was Agostino, the chandler for the Battle of Lepanto: he was struck by an arrow during the battle but died exultant as the Venetians destroyed the Ottoman fleet. The San Polo branch of the family which also lived in the palace also saw two members die in the wars against the Turks in the 1500s but is famous for its precious collection of paintings. The core of the collection comprised 17 canvases by Titian, probably purchased by Cristoforo Barbarigo in 1581 from the son of the painter, Pomponio. Numerous paintings were added to embellish this extraordinary collection: two by Giovanni Bellini and one each by Giorgione, Jacopo Bassano, Tintoretto and Annibale Carracci – as well as many other artists. Unfortunately, the last heir of the family, Giovanni Filippo, in 1794 suffered a terrible tragedy: his only son, Alvise, died as a child in a fire caused by the carelessness of a servant. The disconsolate father died and left the entire inheritance to a distant relative of the Giustinian family, a dissolute character who literally sold everything off. The best part of the collection was purchased by Tsar Nicholas I and is today housed in the halls of the Hermitage in St. Petersburg.

Palazzo Barbaro

The Barbaro family was one of the best-known and prestigious in Venice, despite never boasting even one doge among its many male descendants. The palace named after this family, however, was built in the 1400s by the wealthy Spiera family of "native citizens": this term was used to define families not of noble origins but nevertheless involved in the foundation of the city. Two members of the well-educated Barbaro family left an important mark in humanist literature: Francesco, father of Zaccaria who purchased the palace, and Ermolao, son of Zaccaria, a fine Latin philologist. The family's bond with culture perfectly explains an episode that resembles a tale by Boccaccio, where acumen triumphs over grey moralising: in 1573, the Inquisition put Paolo Veronese on trial, accusing him of irreverence for having painted a Last Supper that was too "festive". The accusation of defamation was extremely serious: the painter had set Jesus and the Apostles against scenes of everyday life in the 1500s: a servant with a nose-bleed, German mercenaries, dwarfs, clowns, dogs and parrots. The Saviour was even served by a black slave! The Serene Republic, however, had no intention of allowing a foreign court to pass judgement in its territory – not even a Papal Court. Venice had to accept the ecclesiastic tribunal but controlled it through a specifically created magistracy – the Heresy Wise Men. That year, the magistrates in question were Jacopo Foscarini, Alvise Zorzi and Marc'Antonio Barbaro, a skilled diplomat. How could they pro-

*In 1885, **Palazzo Barbaro** was purchased by the Curtis family, a wealthy couple from Boston. They were admirers of art and literature, their guests in the palace included Henry James – who described it in "The Wings of the Dove" – and painters John Sargent and Claude Monet.*

tect the great painter and his work, which would have been destroyed if the artist were condemned? The three magistrates found a formula that saved Veronese, the painting (despite a few changes) and the face of the inquisitors: the title of the painting was merely changed from *The Last Supper* to *The House of Levi*. In 1694, the palace was merged with the adjacent building to create a ballroom and the facade was rebuilt by Venetian Antonio Gaspari in a rather staid Baroque style. The ballroom, on the contrary, is much more exuberant, full of stuccos, cupids and other affectations typical of the period. On the other hand, the large library is extremely elegant.

Palazzo Coccina Tiepolo Papadopoli

The Coccina family originated from Bergamo, the last outpost of the Serene Republic on "firm land", grasped from Milan in XV century at the price of four wars and huge financial outlays. They moved to Venice to take closer care of their commercial interests and in the mid-1500s their fortune had grown so much that they decided to reward themselves with a new palace. The project was designed and supervised by Gian Giacomo dei Grigi, a "son of art" born in Bergamo – a fact that was probably decisive for the Coccina family. The palace was completed in 1560 and the family decided to furnish it with accessories worthy of the overall setting: Il Veronese was commissioned to paint four canvases with a religious subject for the noble floor, as well as two paintings by Gian Domenico Tiepolo (*The Minuet* and *The Charlatan*). All these works were later sold to the Este family in 1645 and are today owned by the Gemaldegalerie in Dresden. The building was sold to the Tiepolo family in 1748, when the Coccina family died out. After various changes of ownership, in 1864 it was purchased by the Aldobrandini-Papadopoli Counts, who decided to restore the interiors. Unfortunately, the XIX century was the worst time for such work and the architect engaged imitated all his colleagues of the time: he gutted the rooms and overturned the original ground plan without any respect. The small homes adjacent to the palace were demolished, to make way for the garden, and a new side wing was built behind it. It has been owned since 1922 by the Arrivabene family and is now home to the National Research Council.

Palazzo Contarini delle Figure

It was rebuilt in the early 1500s by Antonio Abbondi, nicknamed Scarpagnino, on the base of a previous Gothic building; the palace owes its name to the two figures in low relief overlooking the gate on the Grand Canal itself, which seem to support – like caryatids – the balcony of the noble floor. Gossip suggested that they depicted the despair of a man who had lost everything at the gambling tables and his furious wife. The wealth

*Just like all the rooms, the Dining Hall in **Palazzo Contarini delle Figure** is also replete with works of art.*

of details in the building – the capitals of the facade were originally gilt with gold – perfectly represent its owner, Jacopo Contarini: he was a man known for his great culture and love of the arts and was engaged by the Serene Republic to select the paintings for the Halls of the Main Council and the Scrutinio, in the Ducal Palace. He collected works by Veronese, Titian, Tintoretto, Palma the Younger and Bassano and was also a close friend of Andrea Palladio, who was a guest here in 1570. Bertucci, the last descendent of this branch of the Contarini family, died in 1713 and following Jacopo's will, all furnishings, works of art and books (175 manuscripts and 1,500 books) were donated to the Serene Republic. Today, they are kept in the Ducal Palace and the Marciana National Library. The building was sold in XIX century to the Marquis from Ravenna, Alessandro Guiccioli. Lord Byron had rented several rooms in the adjacent "Casa Vecchia" Mocenigo Palace and thus met the great love of his life, Teresa Gamba, then the 19 year old wife of the Marquis.

Palazzo Corner "de la Ca' Granda"

The Corner were one of the most powerful noble families that branched into many lines; their mercantile fortune meant they owned many palaces. In order to distinguish them all, the Venetians gave them nicknames – and this building has one that summarises wonder over its sheer dimensions: even a casual glance immediately highlights the enormous difference in size compared to adjacent palaces. The history of its origins is rather curious: in 1532, a fire caused by hot coals under the roof lit to dry a batch of sugar cane, completely destroyed the Malombra palace, the ancient home of the family. Giovanni Corner, as the head of the family, engaged Jacopo Sansovino to design the new palace as a monument to the perennial glory of his noble lineage. He perhaps hoped to see it finished – but he died in 1551, while the palace was only completed at least five years later. His last will and testament gives us an idea of the wealth of such a powerful noble family at the times: three palaces in Venice, villas and estates in the hinterland, shares in numerous companies, cash deposited at the Mint or with banks and, lastly, income from official business in Cyprus: a kind of feud which provided the Corner family with the sugar cane that in the end burnt down their palace. The Corner family also boasts a queen, Caterina, although the decision to wed a young girl of this family to the King of Cyprus was taken by the Serene Republic. When she was widowed, Caterina was "invited" to donate the kingdom to the Serene Republic; in exchange, she was given the purely formal title of Lady of Asolo, a small and delightful town in the Treviso area. In 1812, Nicolò, the last-but-one descendent of the branch owning the palace, sold it to the State, that is to the Na-

poleonic Kingdom of Italy. The interiors were despoiled of furniture and numerous works of art, including paintings by Tintoretto, Raphael and Titian. The Austrians then turned it into the head offices of the Provincial Delegation (Prefecture) and after annexation by the Kingdom of Italy, the building retained this function.

Palazzo Corner Spinelli

The palace was built towards the end of the 1400s by the Lando family, one of the sixteen "new nobles" known as "ducal", because – thanks to a behind-the-scenes agreement – they managed to monopolise the role of doge from 1382 to 1612. This agreement, that eliminated the "old families" from election to the main position in the Serene Republic, did not bring the Lando famliy many advantages, at least in comparison to other aristocratic families: the family boasts only one doge and four procurators of St. Mark. Their palace was designed by Mauro Codussi, who thereby had the chance to experiment with the style that he later fully embodied in the Loredan Vendramin Calergi palace: the design of the huge windows is the same but here the solid parts of the facade are still dominant.

In 1532, Giovanni Corner became "homeless": his palace on the Grand Canal was burnt down overnight by a fire (see Palazzo Corner "de la Ca' Granda") and Pietro Lando, then Archbishop of Candia, sold him this palace. Giovanni, in 1542, engaged Michele Sanmicheli to adapt the interiors of his temporary "little home". Few traces of this restoration remain but we know that one chamber was decorated with as many as nine paintings by Giorgio Vasari, today owned by various museums world-wide (while some have unfortunately been lost). In 1740, the building was purchased by the Spinelli, wealthy silk merchants originally from Castelfranco; after passing into the hands of the Cor-

noldi family, in 1850 it came to be owned by the famous (and disgraceful) *étoile* of Maria Taglioni, the "destroyer" of Ca' d'Oro. However, the dancer did not cause too much damage to this palace – she merely added an entrance staircase with side balusters taken without any restraint precisely from Ca' d'Oro.

The simple facade of Palazzo D'Anna Viaro Martinengo hides sumptuous interiors embellished by an important collection of furniture and ancient paintings.

Palazzo D'Anna Viaro Martinengo

Built in the 1500s for the Florentine Talenti family, it was immediately afterwards purchased by Martino d'Anna, a Flemish merchant who was a friend of Titian. Today it is a rather staid palace with simple outlines but it was originally greatly admired for the beauty of the mythological frescoes decorating the entire facade, the work of Pordenone. An anonymous drawing today owned by the Victoria and Albert Museum in London helps reconstruct the composition: the noble floor had depictions of *Mercury in flight* and *Cibelis on a flying chariot*; above the main door one could admire *The Rape of Persephone*, while between the lower side windows there was *The Rape of the Sabine Women* and *Marcus Curtius in front of the Chasm*. In the 1900s, it was purchased by Giuseppe Volpi di Misurata, father of the chemical industry at Marghera.

*The Rialto Bridge seen from the Grand Canal. The rigorous facade of **Palazzo dei Camerlenghi** is on the right.*

Palazzo dei Camerlenghi

The austere appearance of Palazzo dei Camerlenghi was perfect for its original function: verification of tax revenues. The Camerlenghi de Comun were a financial magistracy of the Serene Republic but even before it housed these officials the building was the head offices of the "Governatori alle Entrade" (tax collectors) who had exactly the same role as the State Inland Revenue in Italy today. As well as the offices of officials, there were also prison cells for tax evaders: people passing by could freely see the prisoners as a reminder of the fate reserved to those who did not pay their taxes. In truth, however, the severity of the facade is not original: when the palace was built, between 1525 and 1528, is was embellished with multi-colour marbles ... that somehow vanished following the end of the Republic. Even the interiors were sumptuous: the nobles called upon to perform public duties customarily left, at the end of their mandates, a gift that recalled them and at the same time embellished the office where they

had worked. The Camerlenghi (chamberlains) and governors, on retirement, left paintings with religious subjects, complete with the coat of arms of their family and their portraits. The chosen painter was the same for all of them: Bonifacio de' Pitati da Verona, together his workshop and assistants. It almost seems as if the office had stipulated an agreement with the painter, as is often still the case in our own times in order to obtain discounts. Over time, then, the interior was enriched by a full-scale pictorial cycle, which was unfortunately lost with the arrival of the Kingdom of Italy in 1806: the canvases were transferred to the Brera Academy and Modena Academy. From here, they travelled to Vienna when Venice was consigned to the Austrians and, lastly, returned home in 1919 following victory in the First World War. Yet their travels were by no means over: some of the canvases are in the Academy and others at the Giorgio Cini Foundation on the island of San Giorgio Maggiore. There are no plans today to return them to the by now bare rooms of the Palazzo dei Camerlenghi, today home to the National Auditing Office.

Palazzo Grimani

Michele Sanmicheli from Verona received the commission for this building in 1561 from Girolamo Grimani, a Procurator of St. Mark. It was built in a monumental, classic style that immediately highlighted the power of the owners and their love of Antiquity (the family's collection of classic works is rightly famous). As ever, the influence of a noble family was linked with its wealth and the Grimani were certainly no exception: the first floor of the building alone cost 2,840 ducats. In 1597, the coronation as "duchess" of the wife of Doge Marino, son and heir of Girolamo who commissioned the palace, was celebrated with incomparable magnificence. The more conservative senators opposed such an immense waste of money to glorify a single family rather than the Republic – but all the others were highly delighted to enjoy such an epoch-making event. Tassini wrote in his chronicles: "Inasmuch, these shores in the late afternoon of 4 May 1597 saw the arrival of the ducal "bucentaur" and "peate" with the Councillors and the other Pregadi nobles and, with the Great chancellor, they all – to the sound of trumpets and the rumble of artillery, climbed the staircases to enter the Hall. Then, the Knight of the Doge went for the Princess, who immediately joined the assembly, made vows to the Ducal Commission and gave a bag of gold to each Councillor and the Great Chancellor. [...] After this ceremony, the "duchess" went aboard a "bucentaur" accompanied by a crowd of boats and brigs of the Guilds all magnificently decorated. She then descended in "Piazzetta di San Marco", where the butchers had set up a great arch, and with all her retinue toured the squares beneath a colonnade of curtains. The entourage

was greeted by 300 bombardiers, holding the standards behind the Guilds; then came the pipe and trumpet players; then came a rank of young noble women, two by two, dressed in white silk, followed by other, older dames dressed in green, purple and pale pink. The noble laides were follo-wed by four lady procurators and the wife of the Great chancellor in a black silk garment. Then came seven of the daughters and nieces of the "duchess" in white, silver and gold attire. At last, preceded by six damsels dressed in green, and two handsome dwarfs – one male, the other fe-male – the "duchess" appeared with a crown on her head, from which a flimsy veil fell to her arms, wearing a white cloak and a petticoat with gold curls. The procession terminated with the Coun-cillors, the Procurators and all the Lords of the city. Thus accompanied, Morosina Morosini entered the Basilica of St. Mark and hence the Ducal Pa-lace, passing before all the 19 Guilds in fine array. On reaching the Main Hall, seated on a throne, a fine feast ensued with dishes prepared from con-serves representing men, women, boats and other objects which, by the light of 60 torches, had first been carried all around St. Mark's Square.

*The history of **Palazzo Grimani** had legendary and fairy-tale beginnings: one of the Grimani asked for the hand of a Tiepolo but her father refused to give his daughter to a man who did not own a palace on the Grand Canal. Grimani there-fore built a palace almost opposite the Tiepolo palace – it was so imposing that its windows were even larger than the main door of the mansion of the man who had rejected him.*

Morosina Morosini became a widow and ended her days in the palace of San Luca on 29 January 1614, affixing to the Basilica of St. Mark the 'Golden Rose' sent to her as a gift by Pope Clement VIII." The palace was acquired in the 1800s by the Austrian Government and today is home to the Appeal Court.

Palazzo Grimani Marcello

Built on the site of a previous Veneto-Byzantine building, perhaps owned by the Giustinian family, this palace was designed in the early 1500s by Giovanni Buora on behalf of the Grimani branch of the family nicknamed "dall'albero d'oro" (tree of gold). The typical Renaissance style is rational and unadorned: a scenario ideal for the meetings organised in the 1700s by Piero Grimani. Piero was Doge 1741-1752 and an admirer of the Enlightenment. His palace thus welcomed meetings dedicated to projects for economic and social reforms. During his time as doge, in 1744, the first stone of the last great public work completed by the Serene Republic was laid: the Murazzi, designed in 1716 by Father Vincenzo Maria Coronelli, the cosmographer of the Serene Republic. This work involved two large underwater walls needed to prevent coastal erosion by high tides. Impressively 14 metres wide by a height of four and a half metres above the average tide level, they are divided into two sections: the Pellestrina Murazzi, four kilometres long and completed in 1751, and the Sottomarina Murazzi, 1,200 metres long and terminated in 1782.

Palazzo Gussoni Grimani della Vida

The ancient and wealthy Gussoni family was already well-known in Venice in XI century. In the mid-1500s, the family decided to give a new look to their palace – in the Gothic style – and

engaged Michele Sanmicheli to conduct the project. In 1731, Giustiniana, the daughter and heiress of the last descendent of the family – Senator Giulio – was on everyone's lips with gossip that caused great concern among the noble families: she eloped with Count Francesco Tassis from Bergamo and claimed they had been secretly married. The Council of Ten did not acknowledge the marriage, Giustiniana was widowed soon after and on her return to Venice married Piero Maria Curti. The palace was sold to the Grimani at the end of the 1700s, who in turn sold it in 1814 to Cesare della Vida, a Jewish businessman. Today it is home to the Veneto Regional Administrative Tribunal.

Palazzo Gussoni Grimani della Vida today is rather anonymous, yet the facade was originally embellished by the frescoes of Jacopo Tintoretto, that time has since cancelled. The scenes depicted were inspired by the sculptures of Michelangelo in the Medici Chapels in Florence.

Palazzo Loredan Vendramin Calergi

The building is one of the first examples of the new Renaissance style and is considered among the finest. It was designed by Mauro Codussi from Bergamo for Andrea Loredan with the precise purpose of exalting the prestige of the noble family. Andrea seems to have been rather a ruffian and the palace soon welcomed a large number of

*Since 1946, **Palazzo Loredan Vendramin Calergi** has been owned by the City of Venice and is now used as the Winter home of the Casinò.*

good-for-nothings. In 1513, at the end of a battle near Vicenza against Imperial and Spanish troops, Loredan was found dead – presumed murdered by a Venetian seeking revenge for a public slap in the face. In the struggle for plunder, his corpse was even decapitated by two soldiers of the Serene Republic. Such disgrace in death seems to have been the just reward for the arrogance demonstrated during his life: although his will forbade the heirs not only to sell but not even to rent the palace, it was leased in 1566 and in 1581 was even sold to the Count of Brunswick. In 1583, the Count sold it to the Gonzaga, but the Dukes of Mantua did not pay him. Six years later, the building was put up for auction and one of its tenants, Vettor Calergi, made the best bid. This nobleman had no direct heirs and the palace was inherited by his nephews – provided that they added their maternal surname to the paternal surname – Grimani. Yet the three Grimani Calergi brothers were quite unpleasant characters. In 1658, after a series of violent acts, they kidnapped their hated rival Francesco Querini Stampalia and murdered him right inside the building. The Council of Ten bani-

shed them from the territories of the Republic, depriving them of their noble titles and all their assets. The wing of the palace built in 1614, where the murder took place, was demolished and the Serene Republic erected in its place a column of shame and disgrace. The three brothers did not actually abandon the Republic of St. Mark: on leaving Venice itself, they sought refuge in their possessions in the Polesine area. In 1660, the Grimani Calergi paid 7,350 ducats to support the expenses of the war against the Turks and were allowed to return. On their return to Venice, the three brothers rebuilt the demolished wing and no one remembered their crime – so much so that Vettor, a son of Giovanni, even became a member of the Council of Ten.

When the Grimani Calergi line died out, the palace in 1739 came into the possession of Nicolò Vendramin, cousin of the last heir, who thereafter took the surname Vendramin Calergi. Richard Wagner died here in 1883 and is remembered by a plaque with an inscription by Gabriele D'Annunzio located on the side of the palace overlooking the garden.

*It seems that **Palazzo Mocenigo "Casa Nuova"** was built in 1454 but there are no longer any traces of the original Gothic style: it was completely renovated in 1579 to provide a worthy welcome to Alvise I Mocenigo, the doge of the victory at Lepanto.*

Palazzo Mocenigo "Casa Nuova"

The attribution of the design is controversial but most experts credit it to Alessandro Vittoria from the Trentino area given its similarities with Palazzo Balbi, almost opposite. The interior is utterly astonishing with the huge atrium and the majestic staircase leading up to the noble floor – evident signs that the palace was designed to host great receptions, as was later the case. One example: in 1716, Pisana Cornaro Mocenigo organised memorable celebrations for Frederick Augustus, then the young Elector of Saxony and King of Poland from 1733 as Frederick Augustus III.

Palazzo Mocenigo "Casa Vecchia"

Built in the early 1400s, Palazzo Mocenigo "Casa Vecchia" is the most ancient of the four palaces making up the properties owned by the Mocenigo next to each other along the Grand Canal. It was precisely the antiquity of this palace compared to the others that gave the branch of the family living here the nickname of "Casa Vecchia" (Old Home). The Mocenigo family boasted as many as seven doges, second in this ranking only to the Contarini but on par with the Badoer family, not to mention 25 Procurators of St. Mark. Their influence was vast and their friendships extremely ramified, so that they naturally often welcomed foreign guests who, however, they did not always repay with due respect and honour. An emblematic example in this regard is Giordano Bruno: Giovanni Mocenigo, who once welcomed Bruno as a guest, in 1592 did nothing to defend him against the accusations of the Inquisition – in fact, it seems that Mocenigo himself denounced and had him arrested. Thirty years later, a guest of one of the smaller palaces in the group was Thomas of Arundel, marshal of England. His wife, Anne of Shrewsbury, hosted a salon popular with international diplomats and ministers, where Venetian noble-

man Antonio Foscarini was a frequent visitor. Foscarini until recently had been the first Ambassador of the Serene Republic to the King of England, James I, so that it was quite understandable that he had become friendly with a number of dignitaries at the English court. At the time, however, Venice was prey to intense spy-hunts: the Serene Republic in 1618 had been threatened by a coup, financed by the Spanish, which had only been prevented thanks to a tip-off.

In a single night, a good number of international mercenaries present in the lagoon, ready to attack the Ducal Palace, "disappeared" in the canals. The revolt was smothered before it even saw the light but the climate remained one of open diffidence to foreigners and the former ambassador was one of the first to pay the consequences: he was arrested by the Council of Ten, accused as a traitor and condemned to a death. Ten months after his execution, he was officially reinstated: it was the first time that the Council of Ten acknowledged such an error. A more enjoyable stay between these walls was certainly enjoyed by Lord Byron, who rented a number of rooms between 1818 and 1819 – as recalled by a marble plaque placed on the facade – when he wrote the first two cantos of *Don Juan*.

Palazzo Mocenigo "Casa Vecchia" was renovated by Francesco Contin in the first half of the 1600s and is famous for having welcomed many illustrious figures.

From Baroque to today

Ca' Pesaro

The absolute masterpiece of Baldassare Longhena, Ca' Pesaro was home to one of the most powerful and wealthy families of the Serene Republic, who arrived in Venice in 1225. The Pesaro family immediately settled in the area where they later built this palace: their old home was known as "the two towers" after the original facade typical of the Venetian-Byzantine period. A second palace saw Giovanni, a future doge who built this palace, involved in a frightful event: he fell as a child from a window, fortunately without consequences. The third and last home was purchased in 1625 with the precise purpose of creating a uniform area large enough the new and enormous palace. Work began under Giovanni, in 1628, a skilled diplomat and doge 1658-1659. He was by no means a modest man: his will required his heir, grandson Leonardo, to erect a funeral monument in the Frari Church and also specified that no less than 12 thousand ducats should be spent on the project! This monument was also designed by Longhena and is still visible. Over and above such "modesty", the Pesaro family hardly trusted others: Giovanni's wife, Lucia Barbarigo, ordered that no will of her's could be considered genuine without a secret code. Longhena died in 1682 while the second floor of the palace was still under construction, although the first floor was already inhabited. Soon after, the grandson and heir Leonardo Pesaro also died and the palace was left unfinished. Work was resumed early in the next century, under the supervision of Antonio Gaspari, a follower of Longhena, and the second floor was completed in 1709. The family died out in the 1800s and the palace passed to the Gradenigo, who rented it to the Armenian Mechitarist

Fathers, who later moved to Palazzo Zenobio. They later sold the palace to Count Bevilacqua from Verona. After she was widowed, the count's wife married General La Masa and arranged for her assets to be incorporated in Opera Bevilacqua La Masa, a foundation dedicated to holding shows for young and promising Venetian artists who had no other means to make their names. In 1889, Duchess Bevilacqua La Masa donated the palace to the city and in 1902 it became home to the Gallery of Modern Art.

*The monumental character of **Ca' Pesaro** is not limited to the facade overlooking the Grand Canal, as is the case for many other palaces: the interior courtyard also displays the desire for "grandeur" of the aristocratic family.*

Palazzo Belloni Battagia

The 1600s for the Serene Republic was the century of economic ruin, caused by the war effort against the Ottoman Empire – and for this reason was also the century of the *"nouveaux riches"*: the Republic needed money and readily sold noble titles for thousands of ducats. While it might be a coincidence, the new nobles building their palaces along the Grand Canal all engaged the same architect, almost as if following a fashion. Baldassare Longhena became the *à la page* artist and ideal for the purposes of the new nobility: his pompous and monumental buildings had to disguise their dubious origins. The Belloni were lawyers and merchants and invested all their money to buy the noble title and build their palace: in 1663, only 20 years after its construction, the family had to rent the premises and retire to a much more modest home. The Belloni then sold the palace to the Battagia, of more ancient noble origins but by no means any more honest: "They also resided in Milan," wrote Tassini, "and rose to the Venetian nobility in 1500 after Pietro Antonio Battagia, guardian of the castle in Cremona, donated the fortress to the Republic. In return he received a home on the Grand Canal, the Montorio Villa near Verona and 26 thousand ducats in cash."

Palazzo Correr Contarini Zorzi

The Correr family, originally from Torcello, was one of the "new families" among the Venetian nobility. They had no doges – but two Procurators of St. Mark – and specialised in hunting and ecclesiastical positions, while accumulating great fortunes and considerable power. Among the many prelates, mention can be made of Angelo, who became Pope in 1406 with the name Gregory XII and personally experienced the last and tumultuous events of the Western schism. He abdicated in 1415, together with his rival Benedict XIII, and the church found in Martin V the Pope who returned the papacy to Rome. In the meantime, however, Angelo had made sure that the four nephews he had made cardinals remained so even under the new Pope. In the 1700s, another Correr, Antonio, became famous in Venice for quite different reasons: he was the last nobleman to refuse to wear a periwig.

Palazzo Giuſtinian Lolin

Giovanni Lolin in 1623 bequeathed this palace to his grandson Giovanni Giustinian, provided that he and his own heirs also adopted the surname of their grandfather – which of course was accepted without problems. Yet the main problem, on the other hand, was its restoration: the family did not have enough money for radical work and therefore decided only to modernise the facade. The task was entrusted to the then young Baldassare Longhena, who merely added a few "embellishments". In the 1800s, it became one of the many owned by the dancer (and collector of historic Venetian palaces) Maria Taglioni; it then passed to Luisa D'Artois, consort of Carlo III Duke of Parma, who died in 1864 of cholera. It was lastly purchased by Venetian banker Ugo Levi who, with his wife Olga, turned it into of the most important musical salons of the period. These rooms often welcomed Gabriele D'Annunzio, who was more interested in the lady of the house than the music. The poet, as ever, gave his new lover a nickname and Olga came to be known as "Venturina", after "avventurina", a very precious type of glass from Mu-

Palazzo Correr Contarini Zorzi was built in XVII century and nicknamed "Ca' dei Cuori" after the coats of arms placed on the two doors providing access from the canal. Its originality lies in the asymmetry of the windows compared to the doors, creating a rather bizarre and off-centre effect.

rano. The two were secret lovers throughout the First World War and their passion is documented in as many as 1200 letters. Their ardent tone was so scandalous that Olga prevented their publication for decades. Today, the palace is home to the "Ugo & Olga Levi" Music Foundation.

Palazzo Grassi

This was the last monumental palace built along the Grand Canal, for one of the last families to join the Venetian nobility. The wealthy, bourgeois Grassi family perhaps originated from Bologna but settled for some time in Chioggia and in 1718 offerred 60 thousand ducats to the Serene Republic in exchange for a noble title. The coffers of the Republic were virtually empty: Francesco Morosini at the end of the previous century had conquered the Peloponnesus – yet this victory proved to be a financial disaster. To cover these expenses, the aristocracy was obliged to open its doors to the wealthy middle class keen to "buy" a noble title. Once they obtained their title, the Grassi also wanted to own a princely palace. Giorgio Massari was commissioned for this project in 1748. The architect was then completing Ca' Rezzonico, on the opposite bank of the Grand Canal, although the two palaces only share the same monumental dimensions: for Palazzo Grassi, Massari did not have to maintain a pre-existing project and designed a much plainer, measured facade that in some way anticipated Neo-Classicism. The Grassi family died out in the first half of the 1800s and the palace later became a hotel and even a resort using water from the Grand Canal. In the 1950s it became home to the International Art and Costume Centre; it was taken over by a group of Venetian industrialists and in 1978 began to host art shows. In 1984, it was purchased by Fiat. The restoration project by Gae Aulenti and Antonio Foscari launched its international visibility thanks to the major

*In the second half of the 1700s, Paolo Antonio Labia decided to extend the already enormous structure of **Palazzo Labia**. The interiors are embellished by a splendid cycle of frescoes by Giambattista Tiepolo set in the precious architecture designed by Giacomo Mengozzi.*

shows and other cultural events hosted in its rooms. In 2006, the palace was sold to François Pinault, owner of a huge industrial group in the fashion and luxury sector, and still today welcomes exceptional artistic and cultural events.

Palazzo Labia

It is said that the Labia family originated in Catalonia, then moved to Avignon, later to Florence and lastly to Venice in the mid-1600s. The Labia paid 300 thousand ducats to be admitted to the Venetian nobility – and then had to build a palace worthy of their new status. Giovan Francesco Labia managed to purchase land at a strategic point – the confluence of the Canal Regio (Cannaregio) and the Grand Canal – so that the palace in fact has three facades: a small one overlooks Canalazzo, the monumental facade faces Canal Regio and a plainer one Campo San Geremia. Modesty was by no means a distinction of this household, so much so that the Venetians soon enjoyed enlightening and legendary gossip: one Labia invited 40 nobles to a banquet and served them all with plates, dishes and glasses in solid gold; after the event, he gathered all these items, leant out of the window and threw them all into the Canal, saying: "Le abia o non le abia, sarò sempre un Labia" (a play of words roughly meaning "Have them or have them not, I'll always be a Labia"). Such arrogant ostentation of wealth and power was typical of the Spanish aristocracy of the times but the sequel of this episode has a truly "Venetian" soul: they had installed nets just under the surface of the water and as soon as their guests had left they sent their servants to reclaim the precious gold-ware! Little is known about the building of this palace and there is still considerable doubt over the attribution of the project: today, it is thought to have been begun by Alessandro Tremignon and completed by Andrea Cominelli. At the end of the century-old history of the powerful Serene Republic, when the wealth of the Labia had diminished – like most of the other noble families – the building was sold. It often changed hands and became a school as well as a popular home divided into apartments. The frescoes first risked being lost through neglect and then following the explosion of a barge full of munitions during the Second World War which caused very serious damage.

After the war, it was acquired by the petroleum magnate and collector Carlos de Beistegui, who halted the deterioration of the frescoes and adorned the palace with ancient furniture and superb Flemish tapestries. In 1964, it was sold to RAI (State TV-Radio): Despite his wealth, Beistegui did not have enough funds to restore the palace; as well as restoration of the works of art, in short, precarious static conditions also needed urgent attention. The public corporation undertook careful restoration of the entire complex and the palace once again boasted all its splendour.

Palazzo Michiel delle Colonne

This palace was probably built by the Grimani in XIII century. In the late-1600s it was acquired by the Zen family and restored by architect Antonio Gaspari in the fashion of the times. In 1707, the last Duke of Mantua, Ferdinando Carlo Gonzaga, fled his home city after its conquest by Imperial troops and settled in this building, which he had purchased shortly beforehand, bringing with him part of his amazing art collection. It changed hands again very soon – the palace was bought by the Michiel family, a legendary house that for centuries had been excluded from power in the Serene Republic. The Michiel family, as was often the case among Venetian nobles, claimed origins from a Roman senator – nevertheless, it was one of the twelve "apostolic" families that in 697 elected the first doge, Paoluccio Anafesto, near Eraclea. The family boasted as many as three doges in just 80 years of history, between the end of the XI and the middle of the XII centuries – a sign that they were extremely powerful in this period. Yet the assumption that doge-ship was a kind of personal and hereditary monarchy, however, was their ruin: two of their three doges were assassinated. Vitale I (1096-1102) was murdered during a popular uprising; Vitale II (1156-1172), on his return from a disastrous naval expedition, was violently accused, sought refuge in the Church of San Zaccaria but was found and killed. Thereafter, the family kept in the background – although Venice, on Thursday before Lent, still celebrates the naval victory of Vitale II over the fleet of the Patriarch of Aquileia which ensured the definitive dominion of the Republic of St. Mark over the Veneto lagoon. In 1716, the palace welcomed Frederick II, then the young Elector of Saxony and soon after elected King of Poland, who was greeted with memorable balls and performances. Another illustrious guest was Charles Albert, Elector of Baviera. Today, after

Palazzo Michiel delle Colonne owes its name to the streamlined columns occupying the entire ground floor – a unique characteristic arising from its Veneto-Byzantine origins.

being owned first by the Martinengo and then by the Donà delle Rose, the palace is the head offices of the Registry Office.

Palazzo Moro-Lin

The palace was built in 1670 to a design by Tuscan painter Sebastiano Mazzoni, who took inspiration Palazzo Pitti in Florence. The linear and composed style effectively suggests a "drawing" rather than "architecture", especially when compared to the palaces built by Longhena in the same period. The owner, Pietro Liberi from Padua, was not only also a painter himself but before moving to Venice led a very adventurous life: he went to Constantinopole while still very young, then moved to Mitilene where he was captured and enslaved by the Turks. He managed to escape, fled to Malta and from here first to Sicily, then to Portugal, Spain and France. After three years in Rome, he returned to his homeland and decided to settle definitively in Venice. The palace was later bought by the Lin family: grocers who had made a fortune and in 1686 paid a fine sum to the Serene Republic to become nobles. On the occasion of the wedding between Gaspare Moro and Isabella Lin, the family had the bright idea of adding another floor for the new couple, thereby altering a fundamental characteristic of the palace: its breadth is out of proportion with its height. In the early 1800s, another painter had a studio here – Francesco Hayez, famous for his canvases with an historic background and his portraits. Subsequently, yet another painter, Ludovico Lipparini, bought almost the entire building and held painting salons attended by artists from all over Europe.

Palazzo Querini Benzon

Entirely anonymous from an architectural point of view, this 1700s palace was nevertheless home to one of the liveliest literary salons of the time, organised by none other than "La biondina in gondoleta" (the blonde in the tiny gondola)! The protagonist of this famous Venetian song really existed – she was Countess Marina Querini Benzon, famous (or infamous) for her "open mind". In 1797, when the French entered Venice, she caused a scandal by dancing half-naked around the Tree of Liberty planted in St. Mark's Square. She was accompanied by poet Ugo Foscolo, not yet disillusioned by the Treaty of Campoformio which soon after handed Venice and its hinterland to the Austrians. As well as Foscolo, the salon of the Countess welcomed Ippolito Pindemonte, Antonio Canova, Thomas Moore, François-René de Chateaubriand and George Byron, who met here the love of his life, Teresa Gamba. Stendhal, another famous guest, wrote that in comparison to the Querini Benzon salon those in Paris were silly and arid.

Palazzo Rezzonico

In 1667, Filippo Bon – a procurator of St. Mark – engaged Baldassare Longhena to design a palace for his family. As was also the case for Ca' Pesaro, Longhena once again gave free rein to his creati-

vity. Filippo Bon, in short, did not ask the great architect to renovate his old homes on Canalazzo – that would have been far too little: he had them all demolished and commissioned the designer to build on their foundations a single palace occupying the same area. The idea was to build a kind of royal court. When Longhena died in 1682, the palace was still not complete: there was only the first floor, where Filippo lived, having miscalculated his accounts; unlike the Pesaro family, which managed to complete their palace in the early 1700s, Filippo had run out of money. In 1750, the family sold the palace to the Rezzonico, a powerful family originally from the Como area. Carlo Aurelio Rezzonico had moved to Venice in the second half of the 1600s and paid 100 thousand ducats in 1687 to be entered in the roll of honour of nobles of the Serene Republic and joined the Main Council. The Bon palace was purchased by Giovanni Battista, Carlo Aurelio's son, who resumed work and quickly finished the project. Eight years later, his son Carlo was elected Pope with the name Clement XIII. The Serene Republic immediately seized this opportunity to strengthen its relationships with the Church and please the new Pope by electing his brother Aurelio as Procurator of St. Mark and bestowing a very rare honour on the family: the hereditary knighthood of the Golden Stole. The Rezzonico – already powerful – became even stronger and soon determined to exploit their power to improve the fortunes of the dynasty: Clement XIII did not take long to appoint his nephew Carlo a Cardinal, the other nephew Lodovico a prince, Giovanni Battista an apostolic proto-notary and Abbondio a Roman senator. A classic example of nepotism that rather clashed with the Allegory of Merit that the Rezzonico had commissioned Tiepolo to paint on the ceiling of one room. The palace hosted many delightful parties: they began with the wedding celebrations for Lodovico and

Faustina Savorgnan and then a feast for the election of Carlo as Pope in 1758; the following year celebrated Aurelio's election as procurator and in 1762 another procurator was greeted: Lodovico, son of the former procurator Aurelio. Power in short leads to more power – only for the family to dilapidate its fortune: all these feasts cost huge amounts of money – and the list also includes a fairy-tale ball in honour of the Duke of York, brother of King George III of England in 1764. The Rezzonico spared no expense – not even for funerals: soon after his election as Pope, Carlo's mother died: her coffin was carried along a pontoon of boats installed all along the Grand Canal to the Mendicanti Church. Abbondio's heirs, the last of the Rezzonico, were forced to sell the palace to pay their debts: this happened in 1810 – the power of the family had lasted barely 50 years. After several changes of ownership, Ca' Rezzonico was acquired by poet Robert Browning, who did not enjoy it long: a year later, a trip to the Lido on a very humid day proved fatal. It was purchased by Venice City Council in 1934 and became the home to the Venetian 1700s Museum.

Palazzo Venier dei Leoni

The Venier were one of the "old families" already nobles before IX century and one of its three doges of Venice, Sebastiano, was the commander of the Venetian contingent in the victorious Battle of Lepanto against the Turks in 1571. In 1749, the family commissioned Lorenzo Boschetti to design and build a magnificent palace, that even surpassed the imposing De La Ca' Granda palace of the Corner family opposite. The architect designed an immense building but for still unknown reasons the project was halted at the first floor; the wooden model of the project still exists and is today in the Correr Museum. The enormous expenditure probably convinced them to interrupt work and the Venier adapted to life in this truncated palace. Behind it, where other rooms were to have been built, there is a magnificent garden: the noble family set up here a menagerie with exotic animals, including the lions that gave the building its name. Among the people who have lived here, mention can be made of Marquess Luisa Casati in the 1920s, who wanted to be "a work of living art": she wore live pythons around her neck and strolled around St. Mark's square with a leopard on a leash, escorted by many black servants. During her stay in Venice, the palace was home to superb and magnificent feasts – but on one particular occasion, the Marquess wanted to achieve even more: she rented St. Mark's Square in its entirety to hold an exclusive carnival festival, with a long cordon of Carabinieri to keep idlers away. It was said that during the night she was carried by gondola wearing only a fur coat. Following such ostentatious decadence, the palace then experienced a period dedicated to the avant-garde: in 1949 it was purchased by Peggy Guggenheim, a young American patron of surrealist, dadaist and abstract artists; she lived here for the rest of her life and filled her rooms with endless numbers of works of art. Peggy had inherited an enormous fortune from her father, who died in the Titanic tragedy in 1912. Thanks to her first husband, dadaist painter Laurence Vail, she experienced in Paris the anti-conformist life of artists who she supported by buying paintings and sculptures. In 1948, she exhibited her collection at the Venice Biennial and fell in love with the city. After unsuccessfully attempting to bequest the collection and the palace to Venice City Council, Peggy Guggenheim donated everything to the Solomon R. Guggenheim Foundation of New York provided that the works remained in Venice and were on show to the public. Since 1980, the palace has been home to the Peggy Guggenheim Collection, one of the most complete collections of art of the first half of the 1900s.

Contents

The age of splendour

Lagoon Gothic

A late Renaissance

From Baroque to today

Printed in January 2009
by EBS Editoriale Bortolazzi-Stei
San Giovanni Lupatoto (Verona)
Italy